Muffins

Fast and Fantastic

SUSAN REIMER

Gould House Publishing

Oxford

MUFFINS: FAST AND FANTASTIC

Published by
Gould House Publishing
1 Gould House
Pusey Lane
Oxford OX1 2NF

Cover photograph by Stephen Oliver

First published in Great Britain 1996
Third printing 1997

British Library Cataloguing in Publication Data
Data available

ISBN 0 9528858 0 8

Printed and bound in Great Britain by
Oxuniprint at Oxford University Press, Walton Street,
Oxford OX2 6DP

TABLE OF CONTENTS

To David, Lydia and Philip
Who, having tested millions of muffins,
are happy to eat millions more.

ACKNOWLEDGEMENTS

Even a small book can incur many debts of gratitude:

I owe my greatest thanks to my husband, David, for believing in this 'little project' and for giving his indefatiguable support especially at the computer.

I am deeply grateful to Stephen Oliver for being so generous with his time and skill as a photographer.

Rombauer and Becker's *Joy of Cooking* was an invaluable source of information which almost always had answers for my questions.

I appreciate the bountiful enthusiasm and helpful comments given by family and friends. This book would not be the same without them.

And special thanks to my Mom for teaching me the joys of fresh baking and much, *much* more.

Introduction

'What do you call these?' I have been asked this many times since moving to Britain from Canada. 'Are they cakes? buns? cookies? overgrown fairy cakes?' 'No,' I reply, 'these are *muffins*.' Muffins have been popular for many years in Canada and the United States. They have proven so versatile that they will appear at any meal of the day and, of course, for snacks. Muffins are deliciously diverse: flavours cover the whole spectrum of sweet to savoury, including fruit, vegetable, chocolate, and even cheese and bacon.

So, what *are* muffins? Muffins are simple to make, quick to bake, and very nutritious—a great alternative to junk food! They have a light cake-like texture and yet they have lower proportions of sugar and fat than most cakes. Crisps and chocolate bars, which dominate the snack scene, are very high in fat and offer little, if any, nutritional value. Muffins, on the other hand, are well-balanced nutritionally and offer a wide variety of delicious options.

Muffins were an integral part of my Canadian lifestyle. Baking them each week to enjoy fresh, as well as to stock the freezer for snacks and lunch-boxes, was a basic part of family routine. This came under threat, however, when we moved to Oxford. Anyone who has had opportunity to cook in both Britain and North America will know that some recipes cannot be simply transferred from one country to another. Frustration grows as favourite recipes fail, time after time, for no apparent reason. Eventually my love of baking, combined with my scientific background, spurred me on to find the answer.

Two main problems emerged. The difference in flour accounts for the majority of 'flops'. You can read more about this under 'Notes on Muffin Making'. Likewise the difference in measurement creates no end of trouble. For instance, most people do not realize that a 'cup' in Britain measures about 10 fluid ounces, whereas a 'cup' in North America is 8 fluid ounces. Compounding this problem, there is also confusion over the word 'ounce'. In North America, 'ounce' is usually assumed to mean 'fluid ounce', as North Americans are accustomed to measuring *all* ingredients by volume. (At the back of this book I have included North American volume equivalents for those who plan to cross the Atlantic or perhaps already live there!)

1

Once the mystery had been unravelled, I began to make muffins again in earnest and was delighted by the interest and enthusiasm shown by new friends, both adults and children alike. I set to work developing and adapting muffin recipes to the British kitchen. Every one of these is a favourite in our home and has been tested many, *many* times. My aim is to give you a delicious and successful introduction to the world of muffins.

Please read the notes on muffin making that follow, gather your ingredients, and enjoy!

Notes on Muffin Making

Measuring and Mixing

Standardized measuring spoons are strongly recommended. All measurements with these spoons are level unless stated otherwise. Also, liquid measurements should be made at eye-level for accuracy.

Muffin mixing is very quick and simple. In fact, the key to successful muffins is to keep the mixing as brief as possible once the wet and dry ingredients are combined. Generally, the dry ingredients are sifted together (or stirred thoroughly with a fork) in one bowl, and the wet ingredients are stirred together in another. (These wet and dry mixtures can be prepared in advance but they must not be combined until *just* before baking, as liquid will activate the baking powder/soda.) The wet mixture is then poured all at one time into the dry, and the two are stirred—not beaten—*just* until combined. This final mixing must be with a spoon, *never* a whisk or electric mixer. It should last only about 20-30 seconds, just until the flour has been fully moistened. Be sure to scrape the bottom and sides of the bowl as you stir, to ensure even mixing. The batter will appear lumpy, but this is normal. Muffin batter should not pour ribbon-like off the spoon, but rather should drop in loose globs. If over-stirred, the gluten in the flour will develop, resulting in a texture that is coarse, tough and full of tunnels.

Ingredients

Flour   *Plain flour* is derived from a 'soft-wheat' grain which results in a fine crumbly texture, making it very desirable for muffin making.

Strong flour, on the other hand, is a 'hard-wheat' flour with a much higher gluten content and is not at all suitable.

Self-raising flour is an acceptable alternative to plain flour. If this is your flour of choice, note the alterations to the amount of baking powder given in each recipe. Do not, however, alter the addition of bicarbonate of soda as it is needed in certain recipes.

Wholemeal flour can be used in place of white flour in either plain or self-raising form. If you enjoy the benefits of wholemeal flour, I would recommend a half-and-half combination to maintain a light texture.

In North America, most recipes are based on *all-purpose flour*, which is a blend of soft and hard wheat. When using British recipe books in North America, use approximately 1 ounce *less* of all-purpose flour than you would plain flour. For example, 9 oz plain flour = 8 oz all-purpose flour. (An alternative is to use *cake and pastry flour*, a soft wheat flour, in the same proportion as plain flour. Unfortunately this flour is usually bleached and over-processed, making it less nutritious.)

Two more points about flour. First, sifting it together with the raising agent and salt will ensure an even distribution and minimize lumps. However, a *thorough* stirring of the dry mixture with a fork will usually suffice. Second, flours differ in how much liquid they will absorb. **You may need to adjust the amount of liquid by a couple of tablespoons if you are finding the batter *too* thick or thin.** (Remember, most muffin batters should drop off the spoon in loose globs.)

Sugar   Sugar is important both for flavour and texture. In muffin baking, I have noticed no difference between fine granulated (caster) and regular white granulated sugar. Brown and white sugars can also be used interchangeably in muffin recipes. You might like to adjust the amount of sugar by an ounce or two.

Butter   Where butter is called for, a suitable margarine can also be used. (Check the label.) For muffins requiring *melted* butter or margarine, I have had equal success using a suitable cooking oil.

Oil   I have specified corn oil as it gives a pleasant, mild flavour in baking. Check the labels of other oils for suitability. Olive oil, for

3

instance, is not suitable for baking because of its strong flavour. Vegetable oil, on the other hand, would be fine.

Milk   Semi-skimmed, skimmed and whole milk all work equally well. Powdered milk is a very economical alternative to fresh milk, with no noticeable difference in flavour when baked. Simply reconstitute as needed.

Eggs   Eggs enhance the texture, rising, and nutritional value of baked foods. These recipes are based on medium (size 3 and 4) eggs, but other sizes should not be a problem for single or half batches. Keep in mind the following approximate measurements when the egg is beaten lightly with a fork:
> a *size 1* egg measures *5 Tablespoons*
> a *size 3* or *4* egg measures *4 Tablespoons* (= 2 fl oz = 60 ml).
> a *size 5* egg measures *3 Tablespoons.*

Wheatgerm and **wheat bran** can be found in all health food shops and in an increasing number of supermarkets. Wheatgerm forms the most nutritious part of the wheat kernel, and is a natural source of folic acid, vitamin E, thiamine and iron. It has a pleasant, mild, slightly nutty flavour. A tablespoon of wheatgerm can be added to any baking for extra nutrition. It is best stored in the refrigerator. Wheat bran is now widely known for its role in maintaining a healthy digestive system.

Baking

For best results use proper muffin tins of either standard or mini-size. A standard muffin cup is about 3 cm deep and 7 cm in diameter across the top. Mini-muffins are fun for parties and smaller appetites. Recipes in this book have been adapted to produce 10-12 standard-size muffins or 36 mini-muffins (or 6 standard plus 12 mini!).

Shallow bun tins are not recommended, as the muffins cannot achieve their correct shape and height. However, if this is all that is available, remember to decrease baking time to about 15-20 minutes. The recipes will produce about 18 muffins of this size.

Prepare your muffin tins either by lining with paper cases of a matching size or by greasing with a solid vegetable fat or margarine. If using grease, allow the baked muffins to cool for several minutes to make removal easier.

The proper muffin shape includes a raised symmetrical top, although not all muffins reach the same height. Very pointy or distorted tops indicate the oven temperature is too hot; a tough, leathery muffin will result. Muffins should be baked in a moderately hot, *preheated* oven. That is 375-400°F (190-200°C) in a conventional oven. For a fan oven, the temperature should be decreased to approximately 170°C and baking times should be slightly shortened as well. With a gas oven, use Gas Mark 5-6 if baking on the middle rack, or Gas Mark 4-5 if baking nearer the top of the oven. Remember, ovens vary in their temperature distribution and accuracy, so you will need to discover what works best with yours. Note also that shiny pans reflect heat and so might require a slightly longer baking time than dark pans.

Standard-size muffins should take about 20-25 minutes to bake in a conventional or gas oven; mini-muffins about 15-20 minutes. Muffins are done when the tops are lightly browned and spring back (or feel quite firm) when touched gently. If your finger leaves an indent, continue baking for another 2-3 minutes and test again. If the muffins require more (or less) than the above times, make appropriate adjustments to your oven temperature for future batches.

Storing and Freezing

Muffins are at their best when freshly baked and still warm. Ideally, any not eaten on the day of baking should be frozen as soon as possible to maintain freshness. (One exception here is the iced Carrot Pineapple muffin which is equally good the next day without freezing.) Muffins freeze very well. Simply cool them to room temperature and freeze in airtight bags or containers—perfect for taking out whenever needed, and in just the right quantity! If freezing is not possible, store muffins in an airtight container and eat within two days.

A frozen muffin, wrapped up in a lunch box in the morning, will be thawed by mid-morning or lunch-time. For instant thawing, microwave unwrapped at Medium for 30-40 seconds. In a conventional oven, heat at 350°F (175°C) for 10-15 minutes (unwrapped for a crusty muffin, wrapped in foil for a soft muffin).

The Basic Muffin

Delicious even in its simplest state, this muffin invites creative variation!

9 oz (250 g) plain flour*
3 tsp (15 ml) baking powder
½ teaspoon (2.5 ml) salt
3 oz (85 g) white granulated sugar
1 egg
8 fl oz (240 ml) milk
3 fl oz (90 ml) corn oil *or* 3 oz (85 g) butter or margarine, melted

1. Prepare muffin tins with liners or grease.
2. Preheat oven to 375-400°F (190-200°C), Gas Mark 5-6.
3. In a large bowl, sift together (or stir thoroughly with a fork): flour, baking powder and salt. Stir in sugar. Make a well in the centre and set aside.
4. In a separate bowl, beat egg lightly with a fork. Stir in milk and oil (or melted butter/margarine).
5. Pour all of liquid ingredients into dry and stir just until combined, scraping sides and bottom of the bowl as you stir. This mixing should take not more than about 20 seconds. Batter will be lumpy, but no dry flour should be visible. Do not over-stir.
6. Fill muffin cups ¾ full (or to the tops for larger muffins). Makes 10-11 standard-size muffins, or 36 mini-size. Bake about 20-25 minutes (15-20 minutes for mini-size). Muffins are done when tops are lightly browned and spring back when touched. If paper cases have not been used, allow muffins to cool for a few minutes to make removal easier. Best served warm, with or without butter.

*For self-raising flour, use only 1 teaspoon (5 ml) baking powder.

Here are some delicious variations of the **Basic Muffin***:*

○ **Almond Poppy Seed Muffins**: Add 2 Tablespoons (30 ml) poppy seeds to the dry ingredients, and 1 teaspoon (5 ml) almond essence to the egg mixture.

○ **Buttermilk Muffins**: *Omit* baking powder and milk. *Substitute* 1 teaspoon (5 ml) bicarbonate of soda and 8 fl oz (240 ml) cultured buttermilk plus 3 Tablespoons (45 ml) water. (Wonderful served warm with jam!)

○ **Chocolate Chip Muffins** are ever-popular. Add 3 oz (85 g) plain chocolate drops (either chopped or left whole) to dry mixture.

○ **Coffee Walnut Muffins:** *Omit* 8 fl oz milk. *Substitute* 6 fl oz (180 ml) strong coffee (cooled) plus 2 fl oz (60 ml) milk. To dry ingredients add about 2 oz (60 g) chopped walnuts. Before baking, sprinkle tops with a mixture of 2 oz (60 g) brown sugar plus ½ teaspoon (2.5 ml) cinnamon.

○ **Cranberry Sauce Muffins:** *Decrease* milk to 4 fl oz (120 ml), and *add* 6 fl oz (180 ml) cranberry sauce (the chunky type) to liquid ingredients. A small amount (about ½ teaspoon) grated lemon or orange rind goes well in these.

○ **Lemon Muffins**: Add 1 teaspoon (5 ml) finely grated lemon rind to wet ingredients. Glaze muffins immediately after baking, with a mixture of 3 oz (85 g) icing sugar, 3-4 teaspoons fresh lemon juice, and ¼ teaspoon lemon rind. (So simple, *so* good!)

○ **Wholemeal Muffins:** *Substitute* wholemeal flour *or* a half-and-half combination of wholemeal and white flour. Remember this can be done for most recipes in this book. The half-and-half version increases nutritional value without compromising lightness.

○ A handful of **raisins, currants, chopped dried fruit,** or **chopped nuts** can be added to any muffin recipe for extra flavour and texture.

Apple Spice Muffins

Always a popular flavour! Adjust the spices as you like. Mixed spice (not to be confused with allspice) is a lovely blend of sweet spices including cinnamon, coriander seed, caraway seed, nutmeg, ginger and cloves.

9 oz (250 g) plain flour*
3 teaspoons (15 ml) baking powder
½ teaspoon (2.5 ml) salt
1½ teaspoons (7.5 ml) mixed spice (*or* try 1½ teaspoons cinnamon
    plus ¼ teaspoon nutmeg and a pinch of ginger and cloves)
4 oz (110 g) white granulated sugar
1 egg
5 fl oz (150 ml) milk
3 fl oz (90 ml) corn oil *or* 3 oz (85 g) butter/margarine, melted
6 oz (170 g) apple (any type), peeled, cored, and finely chopped
A handful of raisins or chopped walnuts (optional)

Optional topping:
2-3 Tablespoons (30-45 ml) soft brown sugar

1. Prepare muffin tins. Preheat oven to 375-400°F (190-200°C).
2. In a large bowl, sift together (or stir well with a fork): flour, baking powder, salt and spice. Stir in sugar. Make a well in centre.
3. In another bowl, beat egg with a fork. Stir in milk, oil (or melted butter) and chopped apple.
4. Pour all of wet mixture into dry. Stir just until combined. (Batter will be thicker than for most muffins—apple releases juice as it cooks.) Fold in raisins/walnuts if using.
5. Spoon immediately into muffin tins. Sprinkle tops with sugar. Makes 10-12 standard-size muffins. Bake about 20-25 minutes, until tops are lightly browned and spring back when touched. Allow to cool slightly to make removal easier.

*With self-raising flour, use 1 teaspoon (5 ml) baking powder.

Apricot Almond Muffins

Toasted almonds and apricots make a wonderful combination...

10 oz (280 g) plain flour*
3 teaspoons (15 ml) baking powder
½ teaspoon (2.5 ml) salt
4 oz (110 g) soft brown sugar
2 oz (60 g) toasted almond flakes (use either ready-toasted or follow
  instructions below)
1 egg
3 fl oz (90 ml) corn oil
10 fl oz (290 ml) milk
1 teaspoon (5 ml) vanilla essence
6 oz (170 g) dried (ready-to-eat) apricots, chopped

1. Prepare muffin tins. Preheat oven to 375-400°F (190-200°C).
2. To toast flaked almonds: spread on a baking sheet and bake about
   4-5 minutes, until lightly browned. Let cool; crumble.
3. In a large bowl, sift together (or stir well with a fork): flour, baking
   powder and salt. Stir in sugar and toasted almonds.
4. In another bowl, beat egg lightly with a fork. Add oil, milk, vanilla
   and chopped apricots.
5. Pour wet ingredients into dry, and stir just until combined. Batter
   will be lumpy, but no dry flour should be visible.
6. Spoon immediately into muffin cups. Makes 12 standard-size
   muffins. Bake about 20-25 minutes. Muffins are done when tops are
   lightly browned and spring back when touched.

Alternatively, try this apricot purée version:
  Place apricots in a saucepan with enough water to cover them.
  Simmer about 15-20 minutes until softened. Pour cooking water
  into a measuring jug up to the 4 fl oz (120 ml) mark and discard the
  rest. Put apricots in a processor or blender with cooking water;
  purée. Add to liquid ingredients, but remember to *decrease* milk to
  6 fl oz (180 ml).

*With self-raising flour, use 1 teaspoon (5 ml) baking powder.

9

Butterscotch Raisin Muffins

Full of flavour and crunch. A real treat...

9 oz (250 g) plain flour*
2 teaspoons (10 ml) baking powder
½ teaspoon (2.5 ml) bicarbonate of soda
½ teaspoon (2.5 ml) salt
1 egg
8 fl oz (240 ml) milk
1-2 teaspoons (5-10 ml) vanilla essence
5 oz (140 g) soft brown *or* white granulated sugar
4 oz (110 g) butter, melted
4-5 oz (110-140 g) raisins
2 oz (60 g) walnuts or pecans, chopped
3-4 Tablespoons (45-60 ml) syrup—Golden, maple or North
American 'corn syrup'—for tops

1. Prepare muffin tins. Preheat oven to 375-400°F (190-200°C).
2. In a large bowl, sift together (or stir well with a fork): flour, baking powder, bicarbonate of soda and salt.
3. In another bowl, beat egg lightly with a fork. Add milk, vanilla, sugar and melted butter.
4. Pour all of wet mixture into dry. Stir just until combined. Batter will be lumpy but no dry flour should be visible. Add raisins and walnuts/pecans during the final strokes.
5. Fill muffin cups ¾ full, or to the top for larger muffins. Makes 10-12. Bake for 20-25 minutes, until tops are lightly browned and spring back when touched. Remove from the oven and immediately drizzle/spread about ½ teaspoon syrup over each muffin while hot.

*If using self-raising flour, *omit* baking powder. Do *not* alter bicarbonate of soda.

Carrot Pineapple Muffins

So moist and delicious, and they don't taste at all like carrots! I've used
much less sugar and oil than standard carrot cake. Try throwing in
a handful of raisins and coconut for a bit of fun!

7 oz (200 g) carrot, peeled and very finely grated
4 fl oz (120 ml) *well-drained* crushed pineapple (or 4 slices, chopped)
9 oz (250 g) plain flour*
1 teaspoon (5 ml) baking powder
1 teaspoon (5 ml) bicarbonate of soda
½ teaspoon (2.5 ml) salt
2 teaspoons (10 ml) ground cinnamon
1 egg
4 oz (110 g) white granulated sugar *or* soft brown sugar
3-4 fl oz (90-120 ml) milk *or* water (amount can vary depending on
    how much juice remains in the pineapple)
4 fl oz (120 ml) corn oil
2 oz (60 g) chopped walnuts

Icing (traditional with carrot cake):
2 oz (60 g) cream cheese, at room temperature
4 oz (110 g) icing sugar
¼ teaspoon (1.2 ml) vanilla essence

1. Prepare muffin tins. Preheat oven to 375-400°F (190-200°C).
2. Prepare grated carrot and crushed pineapple. Set aside.
3. In a large bowl, sift together (or stir thoroughly with a fork): flour,
   baking powder, bicarbonate of soda, salt and cinnamon.
4. In a medium-sized bowl, beat egg with a fork. Add sugar,
   milk/water, and oil. Stir in grated carrot and crushed pineapple.
5. Pour all of wet ingredients into dry. Stir just until fully combined.
   Add walnuts during the final strokes.
6. Spoon into muffin cups. Makes 11-12. Bake for 20-25 minutes, until
   tops feel quite firm. Allow to cool before icing.
7. For icing, use the back of a spoon to blend together softened cream
   cheese, icing sugar and vanilla until smooth. (Add ½ teaspoon milk
   if needed.) Spread on cooled muffins.

*If using self-raising flour, omit baking powder. Do *not* omit
bicarbonate of soda .

13

Cheese Muffins

A delicious savoury muffin.
Perfect snack or accompaniment for a light meal...

9 oz (250 g) plain flour*
3 teaspoons (15 ml) baking powder
½ teaspoon (2.5 ml) salt
4 Tablespoons (60 ml) white granulated sugar
3 oz (85 g) cheddar cheese, grated
1 egg
8 fl oz (240 ml) milk
3 fl oz (90 ml) corn oil *or* 3 oz (85 g) butter or margarine, melted

1. Prepare muffin tins. Preheat oven to 375-400°F (190-200°C).
2. In a large bowl, sift together (or stir thoroughly with a fork): flour, baking powder and salt. Stir in sugar and grated cheese. Make a well in centre.
3. In another bowl, beat egg with a fork. Stir in milk and oil (or melted butter/margarine).
4. Pour all of wet ingredients into dry. Stir *just* until combined. Do not overstir. Batter will be lumpy but no dry flour should be visible.
5. Fill muffin cups ¾ full. Makes 10-12 standard-size muffins. Bake for about 20-25 minutes. Muffins are done when tops are lightly browned and spring back when touched.

Variations:
o **Cheese and Bacon Muffins:** Add about 4 Tablespoons cooked and finely chopped bacon.
o **Cheese and Onion Muffins:** Add about 2 Tablespoons finely chopped onion which has been sautéed in a small amount of butter or oil till translucent (not browned).

*For self-raising flour, only 1 teaspoon (5ml) baking powder is needed.

Chocolate Muffins

Irresistible! And with less sugar and fat than standard chocolate cake...

9 oz (250 g) plain (white) flour*
1 teaspoon (5 ml) baking powder
½ teaspoon (2.5 ml) bicarbonate of soda
½ teaspoon (2.5 ml) salt
4 Tablespoons (60 ml) unsweetened cocoa powder
5 oz (140 g) white granulated sugar
1 egg
8 fl oz (240 ml) milk
3 fl oz (90 ml) corn oil *or* 3 oz (85 g) butter, melted
1 teaspoon (5 ml) vanilla essence
plain chocolate drops, walnuts, or coconut for topping (optional)

1. Prepare muffin tins. Preheat oven to 375-400°F (190-200°C).
2. In a large bowl, sift together flour, baking powder, bicarbonate of soda, salt and cocoa powder. Stir in sugar.
3. In another bowl, beat egg with a fork. Stir in milk, oil and vanilla.
4. Pour all of wet ingredients into dry, and stir until combined. Batter will be lumpy but no dry flour should be visible.
5. Fill muffin cups ¾ full. Sprinkle tops with chocolate drops, walnuts, or coconut (or all three). Makes 10-12 standard-size muffins. Bake for 20-25 minutes, until tops spring back when touched.

Variations:
- **Double Chocolate Muffins**: Add 2-3 oz (60-85 g) plain chocolate drops to dry ingredients. Omit topping.
- **Chocolate Cheesecake Muffins**
    3 oz (85 g) cream cheese, softened
    2 Tablespoons (30 ml) caster (fine granulated) sugar

  Stir together cream cheese and caster sugar. Spoon about 2 Tablespoons chocolate batter into each prepared muffin cup. Drop about a teaspoon of cream cheese filling on top, and then more chocolate batter. Omit topping. Bake as above.

*If using self-raising flour, omit baking powder. Do *not* adjust bicarbonate of soda.

Cocoa Courgette Muffins

Don't let the name put you off! As with carrot muffins, the courgette ("zucchini" in North America) adds moisture (and vitamins) but not flavour. Really good. Honest.

10 oz (280 g) plain flour*
2 teaspoons (10 ml) baking powder
½ teaspoon (2.5 ml) bicarbonate of soda
1 teaspoon (5 ml) salt
1-2 teaspoons (5-10 ml) ground cinnamon
2 Tablespoons (30 ml) unsweetened cocoa powder
1 egg
5 oz (140 g) soft brown sugar
4 fl oz (120 ml) corn oil
2 fl oz (60 ml) milk
2 teaspoons (10 ml) vanilla essence
12 oz (340 g) courgette, finely grated by processor or by hand, which
    will yield about 16 fl oz (450 ml) when packed into a measuring
    jug—do not peel unless you want to avoid green flecks
3 oz (85 g) raisins (optional)

1. Prepare muffin tins. Preheat oven to 375-400°F (190-200° C).
2. In a large bowl, sift together flour, baking powder, bicarbonate of soda, salt, cinnamon and cocoa powder. Set aside.
3. In a medium-sized bowl, beat egg with a fork. Add brown sugar, oil, milk, vanilla and grated courgette. Stir well.
4. Pour all of wet mixture into dry. Stir just until combined, adding raisins in the final strokes. Do not overstir. Batter will be lumpy but no dry flour should be visible.
5. Fill muffin cups ¾ full. Makes 12 standard-size muffins. Bake for about 20-25 minutes. Tops should spring back when touched.

*If using self-raising flour, omit baking powder. Do *not* adjust bicarbonate of soda.

Cornmeal Muffins

So versatile, this muffin can work as a savoury or sweet:
serve warm with butter to accompany a light meal, especially soup or chili,
or serve with butter and syrup to make a tasty dessert...

6 oz (170 g) plain (white) flour*
6 oz (170 g) cornmeal
4 teaspoons (20 ml) baking powder
½ teaspoon (2.5 ml) salt
3 oz (85 g) white granulated sugar
1 egg
9 fl oz (260 ml) milk
3 oz (85 g) butter or margarine, melted

1. Prepare muffin tins. Preheat oven to 375-400°F (190-200°C).
2. In a large bowl, combine flour, cornmeal, baking powder, salt and sugar. Stir thoroughly with a fork. Make a well in centre.
3. In another bowl, beat egg with a fork. Add milk and melted butter.
4. Pour all of wet ingredients into dry. Stir just until combined. Batter will appear lumpy but no dry flour should be visible.
5. Fill muffin cups ¾ full. Makes 11-12 standard-size muffins. Bake for about 20 minutes, until edges appear golden brown and tops spring back when touched.

Variations:
- This recipe also works well in a greased loaf tin or 8-inch (20 cm) square cake tin, and is then called 'Cornbread'. Bake at 400-425°F (200-220°C) for 30-35 minutes. Be sure to test carefully by inserting a cake-tester or toothpick in the centre; it should come out clean with no wetness adhering. (The top can often appear firm and golden while still quite raw underneath.)
- For a different flavour, try adding either 1-2 oz (30-60 g) grated cheddar cheese, or some finely chopped cooked bacon.

*For self-raising flour, use 2 teaspoons (10 ml) baking powder.

Gingerbread Muffins

We especially enjoy these served warm with applesauce or fruit yogurt.

10 oz (280 g) plain flour*
2 teaspoons (10 ml) baking powder
½ teaspoon (2.5 ml) bicarbonate of soda
½ teaspoon (2.5 ml) salt
½ - 1 teaspoon (2.5 - 5 ml) ground ginger
½ teaspoon (2.5 ml) ground cinnamon
1 egg
3 oz (85 g) white granulated sugar
3 fl oz (90 ml) corn oil *or* 3 oz (85 g) butter/margarine, melted
6 Tablespoons (3 fl oz/90 ml) black treacle (see note below)
2 Tablespoons (30 ml) honey
6 fl oz (180 ml) water

1. Prepare muffin tins. Preheat oven to 375-400°F (190-200°C).
2. In a large bowl, sift together flour, baking powder, bicarbonate of soda, salt, ginger and cinnamon.
3. In a separate bowl, beat egg with a fork. Add sugar, oil (or melted butter), black treacle, honey and water, beating with a fork after each addition until well blended.
4. Pour all of wet mixture into dry and stir to combine. This will need slightly more stirring than most muffin batters due to the nature of the treacle/molasses. Break up any large clumps of flour with the back of the spoon. This batter is thinner than most.
5. Spoon immediately into muffin tins. Makes 11-12 muffins. Bake for 20-25 minutes until tops spring back when touched.

Note: Black treacle and molasses are *not* the same. Molasses, a rich source of minerals, gives a stronger flavour in baking. It ranges from the more palatable light table molasses to the more bitter blackstrap molasses. Black treacle, on the other hand, is produced by blending molasses with other syrups, which enhances its flavour but decreases its nutritional value. Where larger quantities are required, as in this recipe, molasses and black treacle cannot be used interchangeably without first altering the raising agent. To use molasses in this recipe, *omit* the baking powder and *increase* bicarbonate of soda to 1 teaspoon (5 ml). This will produce an equally delicious muffin with a darker colour and stronger flavour.

*If using self-raising flour for black treacle muffins, omit baking powder. Do *not* alter bicarbonate of soda.

18

Maple Syrup Muffins

A Canadian classic...and with the goodness of oats!

3 oz (85 g) butter or suitable margarine, softened (not melted)
3 oz (85 g) white granulated sugar
7 oz (200 g) plain flour*
3 teaspoons (15 ml) baking powder
1 teaspoon (5 ml) salt
2 oz (60 g) rolled oats
1-2 oz (30-60 g) chopped pecans or walnuts (optional)
1 egg
5 fl oz (150 ml) milk
3 fl oz (90 ml) pure maple syrup

Glaze:
1 rounded Tablespoon butter or margarine, softened (not melted)
2 oz (60 g) icing sugar
1 Tablespoon (15 ml) maple syrup (plus ½ teaspoon milk if needed)

1. Prepare muffin tins. Preheat oven to 375-400°F (190-200°C).
2. In a large bowl, soften butter with a mixing spoon. Blend in sugar.
3. Sift together (or stir well with a fork): flour, baking powder and salt. Add to butter mixture and mix with a pastry cutter (or rub lightly with fingers) until like fine crumbs. Stir in oats. Add walnuts or pecans, if using. Form a well in centre.
4. In another bowl, beat egg with a fork. Add milk and maple syrup.
5. Pour all of wet ingredients into dry. Stir just until combined; do not overmix. Batter will be lumpy, but no dry flour should be visible.
6. Fill muffin cups ¾ full. Makes 11-12 standard-size muffins. Bake for 20-25 minutes, until tops spring back when touched.
7. Stir glaze ingredients until smooth. Spread thinly on hot muffins.

*For self-raising flour, use 1 teaspoon (5 ml) baking powder.

Oatmeal Yogurt Muffins

*Just as delicious as they are healthy. When available, replace raisins
with fresh cranberries or blueberries for a tasty variation...*

6 oz (170 g) plain flour
1½ teaspoons (7.5 ml) baking powder
½ teaspoon (2.5 ml) salt
3 oz (85 g) rolled oats
8 fl oz (240 ml) plain yogurt
½ teaspoon (2.5 ml) bicarbonate of soda
2 fl oz (60 ml) milk
1 egg, beaten with a fork
4-5 oz (110-140 g) soft brown sugar
3 fl oz (90 ml) corn oil
3-4 oz (85-110 g) raisins (*or* fresh or frozen cranberries or
  blueberries—cranberries should be coarsely chopped)

Optional topping:
3-4 Tablespoons (45-60 ml) soft brown sugar

1. Prepare muffin tins. Preheat oven to 375-400°F (190-200°C).
2. In a medium-sized bowl, sift together (or stir well with a fork):
   flour, baking powder and salt. Set aside.
3. The following should be done just before baking. In a large bowl,
   combine oats, yogurt and bicarbonate of soda. Add milk, egg, sugar
   and oil. Beat together well with a spoon.
4. Add dry ingredients to wet mixture. Stir just until combined, adding
   fruit during the final strokes. Batter will be thick and lumpy but no
   dry flour should be visible.
5. Spoon immediately into tins, filling at least ¾ full. Makes 10-12.
   Sprinkle tops with sugar if desired. Bake for 20-25 minutes, until
   tops are lightly browned and spring back when touched.

Variations:
o Try additional flavourings such as 1 teaspoon (5 ml) vanilla or
  ½ teaspoon (2.5 ml) ground cinnamon.
o These muffins can also be made with milk instead of yogurt. Simply
  omit bicarbonate of soda and *increase* baking powder to 3 teaspoons
  (15 ml). Replace yogurt/milk with 9 fl oz (260 ml) milk in *total*.

Orange Muffins

Fresh orange flavour; delicious with or without the dried fruit...

10 oz (280 g) plain flour*
3 teaspoons (15 ml) baking powder
½ teaspoon (2.5 ml) salt
4 oz (110 g) white granulated sugar
1 egg
3 fl oz (90 ml) corn oil
Finely grated rind of 1 large orange (about 1 Tablespoon/15 ml); be
    careful not to grate into the white pith which is bitter
Juice of 1 orange (approximately 4 fl oz/120 ml) *plus* enough water to
    make a *total* of 9 fl oz (260 ml) — remember to set aside 3-4
    teaspoons if using the glaze
3 oz (85 g) chopped dates, prunes, or raisins (optional)

Optional glaze:
3 oz (85 g) icing sugar
3-4 teaspoons (15-20 ml) orange juice
¼ teaspoon (1.2 ml) grated orange rind

1. Prepare muffin tins. Preheat oven to 375-400°F (190-200°C).
2. In a large bowl, sift together (or stir thoroughly with a fork): flour,
   baking powder and salt. Stir in sugar. Make a well in centre.
3. In a separate bowl, beat egg with a fork. Add oil, orange rind,
   orange juice, and water.
4. Pour all of wet mixture into dry. Stir just until combined, adding
   dried fruit during the final strokes. Batter will be lumpy, but no dry
   flour should be visible.
5. Fill muffin cups ¾ full. Makes 10-12 standard-size muffins. Bake for
   20-25 minutes, until tops are lightly browned and spring back when
   touched. If using glaze, remove muffins promptly onto a plate and
   spread immediately with glaze mixture.

Variation:
❍ **Orange Poppy Seed Muffins**: *Omit* dried fruit; add 1 Tablespoon
   (15 ml) poppy seeds to dry ingredients.

*For self-raising flour, use 1 teaspoon (5 ml) baking powder.

Orange-Date Bran Muffins

Packed with nutrition and flavour... This was created by my English great-aunt living in Canada, and proved to be a favourite for breakfast and snacks throughout my youth. It's still a favourite in our home, for adults and children alike. (Wheat germ is extremely nutritious; try adding a spoonful to all your baking!)

7 oz (200 g) plain wholemeal flour*
2 oz (60 g) natural wheat bran
1½ oz (45 g) wheat germ
1 teaspoon (5 ml) baking powder
1 teaspoon (5 ml) bicarbonate of soda
½ teaspoon (2.5 ml) salt
4 oz (110 g) butter or suitable margarine, softened (not melted)
Finely grated rind of 1 orange (approximately 1 Tablespoon/15 ml) —
    be careful not to grate into the white pith which is bitter
5 oz (140 g) soft brown sugar
1 egg, beaten with a fork
10 fl oz (290 ml) milk
3 oz (85 g) dried dates, chopped (or raisins)

1. Prepare muffin tins, preferably with paper liners as these muffins do tend to stick. Preheat oven to 375-400°F (190-200°C).
2. Combine wholemeal flour, wheat bran, wheat germ, baking powder, bicarbonate of soda and salt. Stir well with a fork.
3. In a large bowl, blend together butter, orange rind and sugar. Add egg gradually, beating well until smooth.
4. Use a minimum of stirring for the following steps: Add half of dry ingredients to butter mixture. When this is mostly incorporated, add all of milk. After a few strokes, add remaining dry ingredients and continue stirring just until evenly blended. Add chopped dates during the final strokes. Batter will be thick.
5. Spoon into muffin cups. Makes 12 standard-size muffins. Bake for 20-25 minutes. Tops should spring back when touched. If liners are not used, cool for several minutes to make removal easier. We enjoy these split and buttered.

*If using self-raising flour, omit baking powder. Do *not* adjust bicarbonate of soda.

Peach or Rhubarb Muffins

A treat at any time of day...

10 oz (280 g) plain flour*
3 teaspoons (15 ml) baking powder
½ teaspoon (2.5 ml) salt
4 oz (110 g) white granulated sugar
1 egg
8 fl oz (240 ml) milk
3 fl oz (90 ml) corn oil
½ teaspoon (2.5 ml) almond essence
6 oz (170 g) peaches or rhubarb, chopped (drain well if using tinned fruit; do *not* thaw if using frozen fruit)

1. Prepare muffin tins. Preheat oven to 375-400°F (190-200°C).
2. In a large bowl, sift together (or stir well with a fork): flour, baking powder and salt. Stir in sugar. Make a well in centre and set aside.
3. In a separate bowl, beat egg with a fork. Mix in milk, oil, almond essence and peaches/rhubarb.
4. Pour all of wet ingredients into dry. Stir just to combine. Batter will be lumpy, but no dry flour should be visible.
5. Spoon immediately into muffin cups. Makes 11-12 standard-size muffins. Bake for 20-25 minutes. Tops should be lightly browned and spring back when touched.

Variation:
o **Peaches and Cream Muffins**
   Omit almond essence. *Add* about ½ teaspoon (2.5 ml) finely grated lemon rind and 4 oz (110 g) cream cheese—regular or 'light', cut into small cubes—to the wet ingredients, along with chopped peaches. Alternatively if your mouth is watering for real cream, simply drizzle it over the basic peach/rhubarb muffin, preferably while fresh and warm.

*With self-raising flour, *decrease* baking powder to 1 teaspoon (5 ml).

Pineapple Muffins

Light and mild. Coconut creates an attractive tasty topping.

10 oz (280 g) plain flour*
3 teaspoons (15 ml) baking powder
½ teaspoon (2.5 ml) salt
3-4 oz (85-110 g) white granulated sugar
1 egg
8 fl oz (240 ml) milk
3 fl oz (90 ml) corn oil
8 fl oz (240 ml) crushed pineapple (drained well *before* measuring)
2 Tablespoons (30 ml) desiccated coconut (optional for topping)

1. Prepare muffin tins. Preheat oven to 375-400°F (190-200°C).
2. In a large bowl, sift together (or stir well with a fork): flour, baking powder and salt. Stir in sugar. Make a well in centre and set aside.
3. In a separate bowl, beat egg with a fork. Add milk, oil and well-drained crushed pineapple.
4. Pour all of wet ingredients into dry. Stir just to combine. Do not overmix. Batter will be lumpy but no dry flour should be visible.
5. Fill muffin cups almost full. Sprinkle coconut over the tops. Makes 12 standard-size muffins. Bake for about 20-25 minutes, until tops are lightly browned and spring back when touched.

HINT: A 400 g tin of *crushed* pineapple contains enough for 1 batch. Press the liquid out of the crushed fruit before using. Alternatively, use about 8 *slices* of pineapple, chopped finely either by hand or in a food processor.

*With self-raising flour, use only 1 teaspoon (5 ml) baking powder.

Summer Fruit Muffins

Originally a blueberry muffin recipe, I've adapted this to the mixed summer fruit so popular in Britain. Enjoy these year-round using frozen berries. Serve plain for a healthy snack or with cream for a mouth-watering dessert!

10 oz (280 g) plain flour*
3 teaspoons (15 ml) baking powder
½ teaspoon (2.5 ml) salt
4-5 oz (110-140 g) white sugar (adjust to taste, depending on fruit)
1 egg
9 fl oz (260 ml) milk
3 fl oz (90 ml) corn oil *or* 3 oz (85 g) butter or margarine, melted
5-6 oz (140-170 g) summer fruit (any 'berries', either alone or in combination: blueberries, raspberries, blackberries, strawberries, redcurrants, blackcurrants, cherries etc.), fresh or frozen—do *not* thaw frozen berries; larger-sized berries should be cut up

1. Prepare muffin tins. Preheat oven to 375-400°F (190-200°C).
2. In a large bowl, sift together (or stir well with a fork): flour, baking powder and salt. Stir in sugar. Make a well in centre and set aside.
3. In a separate bowl, beat egg with a fork. Stir in milk and oil (or melted butter/margarine).
4. Pour all of wet ingredients into dry. Stir just until combined. Gently fold in berries at the end, using only 2-3 strokes.
5. Spoon immediately into muffin cups. Makes 11-12 standard-size muffins. Bake for 20-25 minutes. Frozen fruit will require an extra 4-5 minutes. Muffins are done when tops are lightly browned and spring back when touched.

Variation:
○ **Summer Fruit Sour Cream Muffins**
Prepare as above, but make the following changes to ingredients.
Omit 3 teaspoons baking powder and 9 fl oz milk.
Substitute:
2 teaspoons baking powder plus ½ teaspoon bicarbonate of soda
5 fl oz (150 ml) fresh soured cream plus 5 fl oz (150 ml) milk

*If using self-raising flour, only 1 teaspoon (5 ml) baking powder is needed. Do *not* omit bicarbonate of soda from sour cream muffins.

Appendix for North American Use

Here are the approximate **North American** (N.A.) **volume** equivalents for weights used in this book.

'Cup' on this page refers to the North American size. That is, 1 cup = 8 fluid ounces = 240 ml

When measuring flour by volume, it should be sifted *before* measuring unless it is a presifted flour. Remember also that, even with the most careful measuring, small adjustments to the liquid in a recipe might be necessary as flours differ in their ability to absorb.

Flour
10 oz/280 g = 2 cups sifted plain flour. Use 1¾ cups all-purpose flour.
9 oz/250 g = 1¾ cups sifted plain. Use 1½ cups all-purpose flour.
8 oz/225 g = 1½ cups+1 Tbsp plain. Use 1⅓ cups all-purpose flour.
7 oz/200 g = 1⅓ cups sifted plain. Use 1¼ cups all-purpose flour.
6 oz/170 g = 1¼ cups sifted plain. Use 1 cup all-purpose flour.
5 oz/140 g = 1 cup sifted plain. Use ⅞ cup all-purpose flour.

Sugar
6 oz/170 g **white granulated** or **soft brown** sugar = ¾ cup
5 oz/140 g sugar = ⅔ cup
4 oz/110 g sugar = ½ cup
3 oz/85 g sugar = ⅓ cup
2 oz/60 g sugar = ¼ cup

4 oz/110 g **icing** sugar = ¾ cup confectioner's sugar
3 oz/85 g icing sugar = ½ cup
2 oz/60 g icing sugar = ⅓ cup

Ingredient	Weight	Volume
Almonds, flaked	2 oz/60 g	½ cup
Apple, chopped	6 oz/170 g	¾ cup, packed
Apricots (dried)	6 oz/170 g	1 cup
Butter/Margarine	3-4 oz/85-110 g	⅓ - ½ cup
Carrot, grated	7 oz/200 g	1 cup, packed
Cheddar cheese, grated	3 oz/85 g	1 cup
Chocolate drops	3 oz/85 g	½ cup chocolate chips

26

Cornmeal	6 oz/170 g	1 cup
Courgette/zucchini, grated	12 oz/340 g	2 cups
Dates (dried), chopped	3 oz/85 g	½ cup
Oats	2-3 oz/60-85 g	⅔-1 cup
Peaches or Rhubarb	6 oz/170 g	1¼ cups
Raisins	3-5 oz/85-140 g	½ - 1 cup
Summer fruit	5-6 oz/140-170 g	1 - 1¼ cups
Walnuts/Pecans, chopped	1-2 oz/30-60 g	¼ - ½ cup
Wheat bran	2 oz/60 g	¾ cup
Wheat germ	1½ oz/45 g	½ cup

Further Notes on Measurements

Although many British units of measurement have the same names as North American (N.A.) units, they are not identical. In general, weights are equivalent but volumes are not. Here are some important differences which may prove useful (now or in future!) to some readers.

1 British liquid pint = 20 fluid ounces (fl oz) = 568 ml
1 N.A. liquid pint = 16 fl oz = 472 ml

1 British cup = 10 fl oz = 284 ml
1 N.A. cup = 8 fl oz = 236 ml

1 British fl oz = 28.4 ml
1 N.A. fl oz = 29.5 ml

As the fluid ounce measurements differ only slightly, they are generally considered to be equivalent for the purpose of these recipes, and are rounded off to 30 ml. The difference only becomes significant for larger volumes.

For single batch baking, you can assume:
1 British fl oz = 1 N.A. fl oz = 2 Tablespoons = 30 ml

In both British and N.A. measurements, 1 teaspoon = 5 ml.
Also, 1 Tablespoon = 3 teaspoons = 15 ml

Key to Cover Photograph

1 Orange-Date Bran	7 Orange Poppy Seed
2 Carrot Pineapple	8 Chocolate
3 Chocolate Chip	9 Banana
4 Summer Fruit	10 Maple Syrup
5 Pineapple	11 Bran Yogurt
6 Cornmeal	

Muffins: Fast and Fantastic is available as a fundraiser for schools and other charitable organizations. Please contact the publisher for more information.